THE *Little Book* OF

DRIED FLOWERS

**AN INSPIRING INTRODUCTION TO
SELECTING AND ARRANGING
DRIED FLOWERS**

DEDICATION
For Ginny and Graham,
for their patience!

Editor: Fleur Robertson
Editorial Assistance: Kirsty Wheeler
Original Design Concept: Peter Bridgewater
Design: Stonecastle Graphics Ltd
Production Director: Gerald Hughes
Production: Ruth Arthur, Sally Connolly, Neil Randles
Typesetting: Julie Smith

Published by
CHARTWELL BOOKS, INC.
A Division of **BOOK SALES, INC.**
110 Enterprise Avenue
Secaucus, New Jersey 07094
CLB 3148
© 1993 CLB Publishing Ltd
Godalming, Surrey, England.
Printed and bound in Singapore.
All rights reserved.
ISBN 1 55521 991 8

THE *Little Book* OF
DRIED
FLOWERS

JANICE SEYMOUR

CHARTWELL
BOOKS, INC.

Introduction

Dried flower arranging has reached new heights of popularity in recent years and it is not difficult to understand why. More forgiving of their treatment than fresh flowers and infinitely more durable, dried flowers, in one form or another, have always had a place in the decoration of a home. Today, with new techniques and a wider availability of a variety of exotic flowers, dried flowers have become one of the most fashionable, as well as one of the most attractive ways of adding that special touch.

In the following pages are a host of dried flower ideas, most of which could be confidently attempted by a complete beginner. Innovative and individual, they provide an inspiring introduction to this creative floral pastime.

A Valentine Card

A romantic present for any time of the year, this arrangement naturally lends itself to the celebration of Valentine's Day. As a three-dimensional Valentine "card," it could be presented in a shallow gift box, set on a white tray cloth over red damask in imitation of Victorian paper lace cards. Its elements are uncomplicated: red rosebuds and leaves set off by a gypsophila spray and a full violet bow of textured ribbon. A heart of woven lavender stems can be found in most good dried flower suppliers and is worth the investment, as there are numerous ways it can be used by the imaginative flower arranger. This design, which leaves most of the lavender stems in view, is helped by also having lavender twig binding. Dark green plastic binding, often used on these hearts, would jar in such an arrangement.

Summer Posy

A very pretty gift, this posy of dried flowers is simple to make. It relies for its effect upon the contrasting and complementary colors of the chosen flowers and the final choice of wrapping.

Start with a garnet-like single red rose in a cream peony and wreathe them in cream roses. Work outwards round the posy adding pink and white larkspur, sea lavender sprigs, one or two dark mauve globe thistles to give depth, reddish beige nigella seed pods, golden alchemilla sprays, yellow straw flowers, pink xeranthemums and creamy wild oats. Once the right arrangement has been achieved, tie the stems with string, disguising this with raffia. To finish, swathe the posy in purple and white net, tied with lilac ribbon, for the light, filmy look of summer mists.

A Moss Tree

Enduring and romantic, moss trees echo an age of well-manicured lawns and neatly trimmed trees and hedges. The basic idea can be adapted to provide a variety of styles – here the tree is left with the moss in its natural state, yet spraying it a subtle shade can be effective in a modern room. The careful gilding of choice elements on the tree can give it an expensive or festive air, while the rounded mossy form alone can look superb framed in a window.

14

It is possible to use plaster of Paris to fix a branch – or, in this case, a bundle of branches – into the container, but plasticine serves just as well in the short term. Cover the foundation with moss and glue a dried flower foam ball onto the top of the branches. Pin bun moss round the ball, pressing the pins well in to hide them. Gilded larch cones and bundles of corn stems give a lively, slightly wild feel against the restraint and smoothness of the moss, while the pensive cherub at the base provides a whimsical final touch.

15

Grandma's Picture Frame

With thought, decorating an old picture frame can bring a new dimension to both the frame and the photograph it displays, as is the case here. The sepia photograph's border of pale pink watercolor flowers is taken as the starting point for the arranger's art. With delicate flower heads of rhodanthe glued to a branch of alder, the frame becomes the basis for a corner spray design that echoes the colors of the photograph's border. Tiny alder fruits and green pokers provide accents of dark brown and green, while a cream satin bow and ribbon make for a suitably Victorian touch. A glue gun is an invaluable tool when putting together this arrangement as it allows the lightest of flower placings with the minimum of fixing.

Decorated Gift Boxes

Using dried flowers is a pretty and practical way of decorating a special gift box – and a perfect one, if the gift be more dried flowers!

The secret of success for such a small-space arrangement lies in the simplicity of materials used. Only a few select flowers and leaves in the best condition should be chosen. A perfect autumn leaf, a pair of Chinese lanterns or a few cones still on the twig, one straw flower and a gypsophila spray – whatever is chosen, the colors should always

work well against the wrapping paper.

Use a glue gun to fix the dried flowers or other dried material onto the wrapping paper or card box. Overall, the best look is achieved by using textured paper or card that is free from distracting patterns, leaving the flowers to make the main impression. For very special gifts, a luxurious wrapping of hand-made paper looks marvelous. Ribbons made from natural materials, such as raffia, twine or even just string, can complete such an arrangement beautifully.

19

Pomanders

....

Pomanders, or pom-poms as they are also known, are particularly appealing as Christmas decorations. These two would look fine hanging from the mantelpiece or a large Christmas tree. Both designs are simple, being based around plastic foam balls.

Bay leaves have been glued to the lower one, which is quartered with raffia and topped with tiny gilded mushrooms, fir cones and cloves in the center of a spray of bay leaves and wild oats.

The other is covered in lichen moss, quartered with hazelnuts and finished with a gold shot tartan bow whose colors are also those of the red roses clustered beside it. Finally, bay leaves and lavender give shape to the spray and rose petals emphasize the form of the sphere, bringing out the warm tones of the nuts.

A Candle Nut Basket

The colors of an autumn hedgerow are reflected in this glowing candle basket, a creative idea for brightening a winter's afternoon.

Use lichen-covered twigs and sphagnum moss as the foundation, pushing the moss and twigs into the basket base around the main terracotta flowerpot to secure it, and also around the candles to secure them in the pots wired to the basket sides. Group the nuts into colors and shapes and glue them around the basket to give an impression of profusion. Also with the glue gun, add green hydrangea petals, similar in color to the lichen and moss, and golden raffia bows.

Although ordinary wax candles will serve in this arrangement, beeswax candles are preferable since they continue the rustic theme, their texture emphasizes the roughness of the other materials and their color tones with the raffia bows. They also produce a pleasing scent when burned. One warning, though: take care that nothing but the candles burn when they are lit!

23

Marigold Hat

The French blue polished straw of this summer hat is given a wonderful lift using dried yellow and orange African marigolds and heads of corn. Straw hats are the most obvious choice for decorating as they are economical to buy and straw goes well with dried flowers. Navy is a good color to use, since the contrast it provides with raffia is sure to turn heads.

Decoration starts with a hat band, which can be a textured cotton ribbon, as in this example, or twisted or plaited raffia. Glue the band in place and then add the spray of flowers. The width of the hat brim will dictate the number and size of flowers used – smaller brims require fewer and proportionately smaller flowers for a truly professional look.

Since a hat can come in for buffeting by the wind, it may be preferable to wire the blooms to the brim, rather than simply gluing them there.

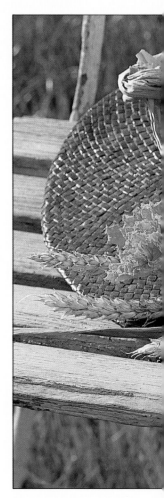

Midsummer Maid

A little girl as a bridesmaid is one of the joys of a wedding, and with dried flowers in her hair garland and bouquet, she is truly eye-catching.

Although not used as frequently as fresh blooms, on such occasions dried flowers have the advantage: they better stand a child's potentially rough treatment and, whatever the weather, they do not wilt.

This matching bouquet and garland both use sea lavender, pink and green pokers, and roses for touches of deep red. The bouquet includes nigella pods, white larkspur, and yellow Achillea millefolium. These are teamed with quaking grass and wired pearls for a delicate effect. Once bound together, the stems are wrapped in silk for the child to hold, with a textured bow to finish.

The garland, based on a wire hoop wrapped with raffia, echoes the bouquet with pink and white rhodanthe. Use a glue gun to fix them.

Rustic Wreaths

One of the most popular dried flower arrangements is the wreath for the door, its timeless warmth serving to welcome visitors all year round. This particular garland uses soft greens and mauves in the form of nigella seed heads, alchemilla and wild thyme. The deep purple lavender is offset by a spray of red roses and a luxurious wired ribbon bow shot through with gold. Placed against the rich color and grain of an antique pine door, these shades show to their best advantage.

There are no rules as to what can be placed on a wreath: after the basic foundation of either a woven cane or stem circle, or a dried flower foam ring, the only limit is the extent of the arranger's imagination. Try attaching not just fir cones, nuts, flower heads, leaves and berries, but speckled egg shells, tiny baskets, cinnamon sticks, dried fungus and shells.

Remember to keep the harmony by balancing colors and shapes all the way round the wreath, with the flowers all facing the same direction.

Hedge Cat

Designed to delight a small child, the Hedge Cat is made purely for the fun of watching a little person discover it hiding smug and snug in the hedgerow, though it is still a garden ornament, not a toy. This mossy pussycat is easy to construct and may even last a season in the garden in a sheltered spot out of the wind.

The basic cat shape is formed in chicken wire, the ears and tail requiring some snipping of the mesh to form rounded tips and lengths. Nothing elaborate need be attempted as simplicity is the key here. Once the shape looks cat-like, add sphagnum moss to the mesh, pinning it with the aid of flower wires made into hairpins.

Give definition to the eyes and nose using small pieces of lichen moss, golden mushrooms and tiny alder catkins, attaching them with a glue gun. Straw for extravagant whiskers and a red bow complete this light-hearted idea.

A Celebration Cake

Of course, any cake can be simply decorated using fresh *or* dried flowers, but for a special occasion, such as a wedding, more elaborate designs are best created with dried flowers as they are so versatile and hardy. Used in the manner depicted here, for example, fresh flowers would soon wilt.

High summer is captured on this celebration cake with quaking grass and pink and creamy larkspur. The creams are accented by the careful use of the stronger gold of solidago, while the pink larkspur is complemented by the occasional rhodanthe and, on the wine glass arrangement, by dyed red grass. Satin ribbon tied around the cake, and cut and curled for the crowning glass confirms the cheerful pink note of the design.

A Venetian Mask

A masked ball or fancy-dress party are ideal opportunities to allow the imagination full rein. For a one-off event, a dried flower decoration to wear doesn't have to be especially practical – indeed, the more flamboyant it is the better!

For a mask such as this one, the starting point should be a simple, commercially available paper mask, or else one made from card. Choose one that covers the nose, or the tickling grasses could prompt an undignified sneeze! Matt gold colored paper provides a more sophisticated background than the shiny alternatives.

Using the mask as the base, cover the surface with laurel leaves, rose petals and greenish blue hydrangea florets. Surround the eye holes with sequins and build up little sprays of quaking grass, corn heads and alder cones above the nose and to the sides of the eyes. Set these off with tiny red roses. Once all is glued in place, discreetly gild the edges of the cones and grasses to finish.

34

Flower Basket

Skilfully arranged, dried flowers can seem fresh. The careful choice of colorful blooms in this design, teamed with sweet-smelling rose pot pourri, brings both the scent and a sense of summer meadows into the home for year-round enjoyment.

Fill a shallow, lined wicker basket with pot pourri, disguising the edges of the liner with lichen moss, pine cones and achillea heads. The moss and achillea are best glued onto the basket, but when attaching pine cones, use

36

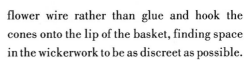

flower wire rather than glue and hook the cones onto the lip of the basket, finding space in the wickerwork to be as discreet as possible.

Place quails eggs in the center of the basket. Use fine flower wire to bind the spray at the top of the handle, which comprises of green and pink pokers, pink larkspur, golden yarrow, long ears of wheat and golden mushrooms. The golden brown tones of the dried mushrooms and the deep pink pokers work well with the rich reds and russets of the pot pourri below.

A Minimalist Arrangement

Stiff dried palm leaves, exotic African seed pods and curled and coiled cane bring texture and movement to this sculptured design. But it is the addition of wired paper tulips that pulls these together in a particularly effective way: an example of how one element can make a great difference to a design's overall appearance.

To achieve this type of look, pick your materials with special care: they will all be highlighted in the final arrangement. On a black lacquer or enamel tray secure a small block of dried oasis and push the various stems into it, hiding the oasis with moss when the arrangement is complete. Consider the stems from various angles, and remember that a design where "less is more" looks best with the simplest of backgrounds.

A Harvest Sheaf

The sheaf of grain, a truly classic arrangement reminiscent of churches during harvest festivals, looks perfect in the window of a country kitchen or set against the dark tones of a summer fireplace. Its simple, harmonious form, using only one type of grain, is especially restful to the eye.

Although constructing a sheaf requires the minimum of tools and materials – the grain, the hessian ribbon or raffia rope and some flower wire – it does require some skill to achieve the essential twist. First, ensure that all the stalks of grain are the same length, trimming them where necessary. Then hold them upright on a flat surface and gently tap them until all the heads of the grain are level. At this point a second pair of hands is useful, for the bunch is to be held securely and also twisted so that the stalks fan out to form the base. Tie with flower wire and then disguise the tie with ribbon or rope as preferred.

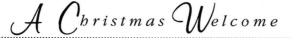

A Christmas Welcome

Garlands are very versatile arrangements, a simple idea that can be dressed up or down as the occasion dictates. For Christmas dressing up is in order, of course. A garland of welcome on an outside gate or door cannot be overly gaudy, however, without looking out of place.

A way to avoid this is shown here, where a touch of gilt in a deep pink wired ribbon and a gold cherub look down on a "waterfall" arrangement of terracotta flowerpots, like Christmas bells in shape but still rustic in feel. The alternative of gold plastic bells, readily available in the shops at Christmas, would look very artificial used here.

These pots are glued onto sprays of Nordic spruce branches and larch cones, which are in turn wired into a pendant of twisted hay. Beside the flowerpots cascade red rose buds, long heads of wheat, quaking grass and raffia bows. The occasional light use of spray snow on the pots and cones provides the final festive touch.

43

Summer's Chandelier

Dripping with antique crystal drops and creamy gold gauze bows, this magical chandelier decoration will add a very special touch of romance to a candle-lit summer ball.

Successful decoration of a chandelier depends upon an appreciation of which dried flowers will show well in dim light – and the careful placing of them so that none are in the way of the candle flames. Here sunny straw flowers have been chosen to pair with rich yellow candles, both showing well beside the gold of the flames. Darker touches are provided by tiny larch cones and dyed red gypsophila flowers – these team well with a deep red crimped ribbon that trails from candle to candle. Quaking grass and raffia bows, as fragile as the crystal drops around them, bring delicacy to the arrangement.

A Rococo Vase

A vase in the form of a small, dark cherub, was the inspiration for this richly gilded arrangement, which unashamedly harks back to the seventeenth and eighteenth centuries and the flower paintings of the old masters. The design bursts forth from its center, radiating outwards in all directions, its distinctive tones of gold, green and brown are both eye-catching and enduring.

Laurel leaves, plane tree catkins, alder branches and fir cones are at the heart of this arrangement, each having been gilded using a brush rather than a spray can for a delicate effect. Protea and a globe artichoke hold the center, while wheat defines the edge of the design. Though this is a formal piece, there is a mischievous sense of the countryside here!

A Celebration Garland

For a truly wonderful occasion that deserves a grand gesture, the overall effect of a magnificent garland such as this is well worth the time and effort of its construction.

For the central swag and the pendants, bind fat sausages of hay together with wire or string, working with them in a hanging position to gain a better idea of the finished look. If a really large swag is contemplated, consider instead molding chicken wire around dried flower foam to make the base.

The central arrangement of gilded artichoke hearts, large fungi, proteas and a sea shell set against a burst of wheat, roses and lavender can

48

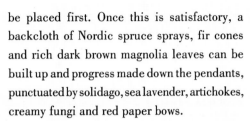

be placed first. Once this is satisfactory, a backcloth of Nordic spruce sprays, fir cones and rich dark brown magnolia leaves can be built up and progress made down the pendants, punctuated by solidago, sea lavender, artichokes, creamy fungi and red paper bows.

Some materials have to be taped and wired together before being hooked successfully into the hay or foam; leaves with very short stems and the paper bows, for example. Heavy items, such as the globe artichokes, should be wired into the chicken wire or right round the hay.

Finally, don't forget to wire into the design the means to fix the garland to its final showplace!

49

The Dried Flower Garden

Easy-to-Grow Annuals

It is easy to grow a great variety of flowers to be dried and used in arrangements. Home-grown flowers can be chosen to match the colors of the rooms in which arrangements will stand and they are more economic than shop-bought blooms. Should the beginner not want to use large areas of the garden at first, annuals, grown for just a season, are the answer.

Possibly the most popular half-hardy annual to grow for drying is the everlasting straw flower, helichrysum. Available in many colors, from russet to pale pink and cream, straw flowers bring a cheerful rotundity to an arrangement. Harvest them when the buds have only just started to break, as they will continue to open for several days after picking.

Another favorite for the beginner to grow is delicate nigella – also a half-hardy annual – which comes in pinks, blues and creamy whites.

Both the flowers and their distinctive seed pods are good for arranging – the pods are virtually dry when it comes to harvesting.

For crimson in an arrangement, try the hardy annual amaranthus, better known as love-lies-bleeding. It flowers in mid to late summer and is best used in its short form, *Amaranthus paniculatus*. Bright orange, to contrast, is provided by African marigolds: the flowers shrink when dried but still hold their color very well.

Quaking grass is a hardy annual that does well on dry, poor soil. The short-stemmed seed heads dry themselves, turning a fine cream.

Finally, every foray into growing flowers for drying should include larkspur and statice. Both are easily grown in a sunny spot and provide a good selection of colors: larkspur being pale and dark blue, mauve, pink and creamy white and statice ranging from these colors through to yellow and apricot too.

The Dried Flower Garden

Easy-to-Grow Perennials

For the arranger who wants a yearly supply of flowers, planting some of the following easy-to-grow perennials makes sense. The initial cost of the plant or seed is quickly recouped and is a wise investment for the dried flower enthusiast.

A good range of yellows for arrangements is provided by the achillea family, golden yarrow being the most commonly grown. These plants do well in full sun and can be harvested in late summer. They dry easily.

Dried delphiniums will provide deep blues on tall stems for grand arrangements, while the more subtly colored lavender dries perfectly and is worth a place in any garden. Sea lavender provides tiny white flowers in its second summer. Invaluable as a background filler in a delicate design, it is easy to cultivate, tough and forgiving of poor soil.

Seed heads are nearly always simple to grow and the most spectacular ones of all – the startlingly bright Chinese lanterns – are great fun to see in autumn. They grow best in a well-drained, sunny spot, out of strong winds.

Finally, no arranger should miss growing roses, since these are some of the most costly dried flowers to buy. Growing roses for this purpose can be very satisfying, particularly as dried roses keep their color and form extremely well.

Drying and Hanging Flowers

Following some simple rules, it is not difficult to dry your own fresh flowers naturally. Pick the flowers to be dried during dry weather. Wait until the dew has left them, usually around noon. Most importantly, harvest them just as they are emerging from bud. Keep them in small bunches secured by a rubber band and hang them upside down in a warm, dry room out of direct sunlight and away from moisture. Only a few flower types, such as hydrangeas, and seed pods, such as Chinese lanterns, prefer to be dried upright. Most flowers take up to four weeks to dry completely – when they are ready, the stems will be bone dry, and it will be possible to snap them beneath the rubber band. If in doubt, leave the bunch a little longer: a not-quite-dry flower's head will droop!

Other methods of drying using silica gel, glycerine and a microwave oven can be extremely successful and the serious dried flower enthusiast is encouraged to investigate these ways, particularly for preserving more delicate flowers.

Tools

It is not necessary to have a lot of equipment to make a success of dried flower arranging. Very effective results are possible with only a few tools, but these few are essential.

You will need a good pair of scissors and maybe some secateurs for trimming thick stems. Sticky tape and florist's wire for binding and fixing flowers, and dried flower foam for holding the flowers in place in a container are invaluable. Wire mesh is useful to hold the foam together on the bigger displays, and masking tape is necessary to hold the foam to the base to prevent a top-heavy arrangement from tipping over.

Finally, even the semi-serious dried flower arranger should consider purchasing a glue gun, probably the single most useful tool for this hobby. A glue gun provides hot, fast-drying glue wherever it is desired in the arrangement, securing delicate flowers in awkward places instantly, with the minimum of effort and trouble.

Containers

Just as in fresh flower designs, the container used in a dried flower arrangement can be crucial to the final look. Indeed, often an idea for an arrangement starts with the container: it is worth investing in distinctive examples.

Natural materials, such as wood, paper, wicker, straw and terracotta lend themselves as containers for dried flowers, as they complement the texture of the flowers. Self-colored metal can look cold and harsh against fresh flowers, but well-chosen dried flowers accompany it sympathetically, often looking sophisticated. Clear glass can be used to contain dried flowers in their entirety, something rarely possible with fresh flowers that need a constant water source. Indeed, dried flowers can be arranged in a much greater variety of containers than fresh ones: receptacles that would look marvelous holding blooms but which would leak or are just too valuable to be filled with water, even if lined, can be used to stunning effect with dried flowers.

57

Dried Flower Colour Guide

White and Cream

Pearl everlasting (*Anaphalis margaritacea*)
Baby's breath (*Gypsophila paniculata*)
Feverfew (*Matricaria*)
Sea lavender (*Limonium tataricum dumosum*)
Honesty seed pods (*Lunaria*)
Sneezewort (*Achillea ptarmica*)

Yellow

Dill (*Anethum graveolens*)
Yarrow (*Achillea millefolium*)
Golden rod (*Solidago canadensis*)
Senecio (*Senecio greyi*)
African marigold (*Tagetes erecta*)
Jew's mallow (*Kerria japonica*)
Maize (*Zea mays*)

Pink

Ice plant (*Sedum spectabile*)
Campion (*Silene pendula*)
Love-lies-bleeding (*Amaranthus paniculatus*)
Barbigera (*Protea barbigera*)
Pink poker (*Limonium suworowii*)
Red bonnie (*Helipterum*)
Festuca grass (*Festuca glauca*)
Pink cardoon (*Cynara*)
Bell heather (*Erica cinerea*)

Mauve/Blue

Monkshood (*Anconitum ranunculaceae*)
Leek head (*Allium porrum*)
Cornflower (*Centaurea cyanus*)
Globe thistle (*Echinops banaticus*)
Sea holly (*Eryngium maritimum*)
Lavender (*Lavandula officinalis*)
Salvia (*Salvia labiatae*)

Flowers available in various colors

Larkspur (*Delphinium consolida*)
Delphinium (*Delphinium elatum*)
Rose (*Rosa*)
Straw flower (*Helichrysum bracteatum monstrosum*)
Statice (*Limonium sinuatum*)
Stock (*Matthiola*)
Peony (*Paeonia lactiflora*)
Hydrangea (*Hydrangea paniculata*)
Love-in-a-mist (*Nigella damascena*)
Chrysanthemum (*Chrysanthemum*)
Hollyhock (*Althaea rosea*)

Acknowledgements

....

The publishers thank the following for reproduction permission:

FINE ART PHOTOGRAPHIC, London, for *Flower Girl*/De Blaas, p. 52.

THE GARDEN PICTURE LIBRARY, London, for the back flap and pp. 8-9 (both Linda Burgess).

JOHN GLOVER for p. 13; p. 28; p. 29; pp. 50-51 and p. 55.

The author would like to thank the following:

SECRETTS LTD, Godalming, Surrey and THE ROUNDHOUSE, Hascombe, Surrey for their assistance in the selection of dried flowers

MRS MARY SEYMOUR for making the cake for "Celebration Cake"

MRS JANE THORNE for designing and making the model's dress for "Midsummer Maid"

MISS LUCY THORNE for modeling the head garland and bouquet for "Midsummer Maid"

MRS KRISS COONEY for the loan of the antique crystal drops for "Summer's Chandelier"